ACKNOWLEDGMENTS

These magazines have previously published the following poems:

Drunken Boat: "Ash Grove of Ash"
Paris Review: "Cast Stones," "Cutworm," "Swing Set, 1972"
Ploughshares (Sherman Alexie, ed.): "104°"
Southwest Review: "Sioux Gone, No One's Home"
Western Humanities Review: "Flame Paper," "Presents," "Smale
    Byrdys Y-Stwde," "Summer Chapel," "Quaking Aspen"
Texas Review: "Thaw"

The recipe in "Smale Byrdys Y-Stwde" was taken from *The Seven
Centuries Cookbook: From Richard II to Elizabeth II* (Maxine
McKendry, ed. Arabella Boxer. United Kingdom: McGraw-Hill
Book Co., © 1973).

Many thanks to Richard Howard, Marie Ponsot, and the com-
munity of poets and lovers of poems at Columbia, all of whom
helped steer this enterprise to its present berth; the editors of the
above-mentioned journals; Elisabeth Frost and Poets Out Loud;
Fordham University Press; and especially my parents, Jim and
Rosemary Sheehan, and husband, John Thorsen Jr.

INTRODUCTION
Marie Ponsot

These poems by Julie Sheehan are a delight, as you can see. In theme, event, décor, and population, they introduce themselves well. Though I want to stay out of your light as you read, yet I think I owe them a few sentences in celebration of their boldness.

Readers and writers of poetry are, like myself, amorous of language and revel in the American privilege of richly mixed dictum. Sheehan dramatically enlarges our sense of what's possible. Her borderless, expansive landscape of language keeps opening outward, seamlessly. The skilled and easy colloquial American English of her poems even takes in the wit and music of Elizabethan poetry. These verbal strategies, forbidden and absent from contemporary poetry, are familiar to us—at least, as echoes—from Shakespeare and the King James Bible.

Julie Sheehan, in the best of her discoveries, melts the icy barriers against them. She simply refuses to deny us any of the joyful fluency of our all-time, polyglot language.

She has, therefore, a wildly good time as discoverer and maker and worker of these poems. I leave you to them, confident that you will, too.

THAW

i

GARDINERS LANDING
(Love Song from Later in Life)

Some quiet night, once you've forgotten passion,
drive down the lane to Gardiners Landing. Pull up
edgewise. The Buick's headlights rest on water,

laid out like fishline. These become your arms.
Watch them, how they grapple the slipping tide,
twin ripple-marks unreeling tempered light.

And if the moon is full of silver, your palms
cool and empty, I promise, you will see
a burst of tiny fishes in the roil.

(In headlit radiance they sting my eyes;
they weave from light to darkness, changeable,
mercury-quick; they dip and fleck in the night.)

Contemplate these minnows, manifold,
kinetic, flashing now, now finning ink,
yet bound up in one mass magnificence—

oh, molecules, mere molecules, but you
held them once, these vanished seethers, bright
on the verge of boiling over the silver verge.

FOR A MOTHER AND DAUGHTER

Of conversations not had; of the mother, who both propagates
and hides her wisdom, mistaking it for pain;
of the daughter; of her cultivation by the mother;
of what the daughter receives and does not receive in the garden
of family;
of frost or drought, and protection from frost and drought
I sing.
I enumerate the fruit and leaves, I record the rhizomatous
dialogue
(it is only loosely covered by dirt),
I pierce the shadow offspring of the living,
of procreation I urge disclosure.

And first there was a woman, and her name was not Eve,
    but Rosemary,
After the tansy dew of the sea, refreshing and impotable.

Canto One

Of the woman Rosemary giving herself first to the man;
of the nuptials and proper bliss;
of the secret shock that she is the invaded one;
of the riddle of her deep receptivity, that it will silence and haunt
  her until some later time.

Lo! on your wedding day you know only how to boil a potato,
  and the words to some prayers.
And lo! the long first day of your marriage,
How he goes away to work,
How the house grows emptier and emptier, distending belly-like,
And how full of demands is the house.
It says *feed me, fill me up with thy wisdom!*
And the oven taunts you with its cold hollows, for you are not
  familiar in its ways.
It is like unto a loaf of bread dough, raw, mysterious,
  bloated with alien power.
You cannot unriddle it, this oven, it is too cold, its pilot light
  too elusive.

And you boil potatoes that day, and serve them, and cannot eat
  they are so plain and unremarkable,
And you boil potatoes the next day as well, and the day after,
  and are afraid to ask for assistance.

And lo! on the fourth day wordless
He presents you with a cookbook as a token,
  and you are ashamed.

Canto Two

Of instincts and their alleged innateness;
of the hospital where a daughter was born in a tornado;
of the bitterness that took the mother at the moment of naming
that which had made her big and empty
and how she chose Pierson, the town that had trapped her.

For lo! here is the nurse bringing you your child!
For although she enters quietly, she is not expected, and you start
and gasp, and your breath hurts in its cavities.
And she places the bundle at your side; she retreats backward,
as if a courtier.
And the air is expectant, the empty room is expectant also,
The quietude demands some expert act on your part;
For lo! your failure has begun again; you know not what to do,
and you do nothing, for fear of harming or violation
And only later does the nurse return, inquiring *have you fed her,*
have you fed her
and you understand,
And even then you do not know how hungry I will be.

CANTO THREE

Of the seeding of knowledge; of its uneven emergence in the child;
of the punishing truths impressed by others without
the mother's knowing.

And lo! I am in the backseat with my brother,
    and the radio is on,
    and we are returning from the grandmother's house
And it is night, and the night licks the back roads, and the car
    slides in and out of the back roads with ease,
And you sit in the front seat, looking back toward us.
And we see the momentousness on your face and we fall out of
    all chatter,
For the night is desolation now, the car is our camp
    and the light from the radio is our campfire;
We attend the passage of lore.

You speak quietly above the radio; you explain quietly the coming
    of babies.
We receive your incantations, the man's penis, the woman's
    vagina
And lo! we are appalled and scream horribly.
And the radio has continued all the while,
    and it is Neil Armstrong,
    and he walks upon the silver dust of the moon.
I look up at the moon, and lo! I see him, tiny and obdurate against
    the effulgent disc.

And I go to school the next day, ambassador of adult knowledge
    and tell Greg DeJong the solemn news
And lo! he falls down not, nor is he amazed, but turns white
    with rage and pushes me upon the gravel
        for speaking of it
    and accepts not the truth from my mouth
And I cannot explain his hate, nor can I tell of my
    harrowed knees,

For although I am possessed of knowledge,
  yet is the utterance thereof forbidden;
All understanding of these things is denied me.

I know only of the man's penis, and the woman's vagina.

Canto Four

Of cool shades of character offered by the mother
through her habits, her clothes, her choice of birthday gifts;
of the general pith as against the growing of roses,
against a fussy perfection most trying,
a beauty induced only at great cost, else unattainable.

Lo! it is quiet in the basement, where I am installed with my new
    tool box,
And the quiet is good, but perhaps too profound.
And you creep down the stairs, not willing to dislodge the quiet,
    for it is rare as a praying mantis,
And lo! I am playing Fairy Princess with the toolbox,
And the wrench is become an evil queen, the king-saw oblivious,
    the slender hammer curtseys in her sandpaper gown,
And the toolbox is become a castle, red as a flourishing rose.

CANTO FIVE

Of dating; of the lies that surround it like mulch;
of the daughter's rebellion, that she may test the mother;
of the mother's silence regarding the lies, that she may let fall
the petals of what truly she perceiveth.

And lo! it is the morning!
And here am I, returning home from the night before;
    the dawn has stricken, white with panic,
And my story is polished, practiced, and stands whole
    upon my tongue:
How I traveled from movie theater most promptly and chaste,
How the car broke mightily, and fell cold upon the roadside,
    and mute,
    and mired itself in freakish mud upon the roadside,
How I fell asleep thus, and thus he fell asleep, not touching,
How thus both of us fell victims to suspicion,
    though we claim no part of the touching:
Yea, verily, will I cling to my innocence like infant to the breast.

And lo! you appeareth at the doorway, quaking mightily.
Your brows are thick with rage, your teeth flash and gnaw,
    your face whitens as unto the panicky dawn.

And I stretch open my mouth, to release my invention,
And lo! my date-clothes speak the truth; they spill forth their tale
    unbidden:
How I drank the pink champagne, how I threw up the pink
    champagne, how I fell cold and mute, mired in
    the pink champagne,
How my date awoke, stricken with dawn,
How he understood not the style of my sweater, no!
    nor the drape of its cowl neck,
For in the sloppy haste of dressing, it came upon me backward;
    the cowl now trails my back.

10

In this, the morning after, in my sixteenth year, do my clothes
    silently speak,
And my invention rolls not out from upon my stone tongue
And you speak not either, but stare most fixedly upon me.
And I stare also, twitch my bright rags,
    fall mute in my false verve.

Canto Six

Of the clenched buds of the mother, that she will betray no fear
in the presence of the child.

And lo! it is many years later, and I visit from the college
And we drive to the city to go shopping, we two, alone.

And now the years of wear, the rutting, streaks, erosion
    of wifehood give out a rusty sob
And lo! you are crying;
The sound is that of a grackle in a minor key.
And I reach over from the driver's seat
    to pat your strange shoulder,
For I have never comforted you and know not what to do
And you shrink back and swat my hand away,
    and I comfort you not.

Canto Seven

*Of late growth and flowerings, and other impracticalities of life;
of whimsy; of sublime idiocy;
of our foolish desire to keep them buried unto this very day.*

For lo! how you once let slip
Your lust for a Mercedes SL500 convertible sports car,
        red,
And how the extravagance now lies within your reach,
For you have learned the ways of men in the agora, and yourself
        become a player in the agora.
You have grasped the tendrils and roots of commerce,
And it has yielded its wealth.
Lo! how you would grasp too your secret desires if you could but
        open your fist.

You cannot open your fist now, it has grown solid, a potato,
Your fingers are undifferentiated, your character is congealed
        and will not amaze me
(Except your eyes, which may yet swerve).

For lo! how the conversations of the mother and the daughter
        are of the wisdom of success only,
And therefore are their bonds forged of public ore,
For the soil of discourse has too much of the apparent good,
The sun beats down its triumphant exposure,
For lo! how we have rooted out the humid air, discarding
        all the sweet methane of folly.
While it rises behind us, the failure of living, fulsome
        and glorious,
We kick clods from the clutches of rakes.

FLAME PAPER

It goes up fast and punishingly bright,
comes in blue-green-orange, but not for long—
(I didn't mean to fight with you last night)

you know the stuff? Magicians' favored sleight,
it hides left hands while right ones play along.
It goes up fast and punishingly bright.

Desperate for a gasp, a bad playwright
might use it, or a gun, or girl-in-thong.
I didn't mean to fight with you last night,

to spur you, raging, ever more uptight,
but you were most spectacularly wrong.
I go up fast and punishingly bright

at cockily lax, knee-jerk, McCarthyite
stabs like yours—pin prickles! paper prongs!
I didn't mean to fight with you last night.

(P.S.: you're holding poor-man's dynamite.
Read it and poof! our truce flames out—it's gone
gone, gone up fast and punishingly bright.)
I didn't mean to fight with you last night.

CARDINALS ON KAUAI
(Nursery Rhyme for Later in Life)

They were everywhere the year you weren't born.
Big ones in dirty blurs, their signals barely

evident, zipping like misfired flares
or treed in green tangles, aborted kites.

Then the little gray ones, pert and trim,
wearing their red like executioners' hoods.

One outright bird hopping on the lawn
I taught to thieve corn chips from the lanai

and watched him. That beak could crack a safe.
It never rained. The temperature was steady.

But something hinges on a cardinal:
I waited like the dirt there, which is red,

red as the tang of chemotherapy.
The plants take to it like their own blood.

SWING SET, 1972

I

Although I am a mother's age, let me fling my legs high,
    dear father:
Let me swoop backward out of the depths,
Let me shriek in the wind like a kite, let my free-fall sizzle
    in my ears,
Let me never outgrow the swing.
And I am dust, and afraid,
But let me hang whole at the horizon's elastic string,
    in the cat's cradle, taut and simple as declamation.

Dear father, you have returned to picture books.
I have seen you curl up with Delight, who sleeps late
    while the young men work.
(If they could, they would use her as broom, mop
    and bucket, these young men.
They would sponge the bitter aftertaste of industry
    with her,
Rid themselves of its ink, soot, slag, dregs, scum,
    dross, offal and scourings,
Deny the traces of the butchered ox,
Deny the greatcoat's scraps,
Deny electricity its eerie water.)

Delight is too sound, though; she sleeps fast,
    inviolate in her dormancy.
The thought of work cannot vex her.
No young men touch her.

But you, my father, too old for work, intrigue Delight
    down to your idle fingers:
There you stand an hour at the mirror, marveling at the
    movements of loose skin.
There you gaze on your kitchen table, how many forearms
    it has gladly received.
You have brought your head to the lowest zone, where the
    insects savage jungle grass.
You have examined the cranberry juice and found it wanting
    not at all.

II

How long ago was it you went to the water to scatter the ashes,
    the shavings of your marriage?
(Her ashes did not rest easy in that urn, for it did not contain
    her shape.)

Together we went, on an overcast day.
We left the ground to the proud fumes of diesel.
We traversed the chopped façade of Manhasset.
You scattered her ashes far out on the water, away from
    the shoreline; the wavelets inhaled them.
You rested your hands on delirious waters.

Dead silent then the long way in,
Dead silent the boatman who took us out, not knowing
    your purpose.
He would not let you pay him afterward, but recognized
    your delight, that you had left all consequence behind,
And what had been terrible to remain was now
    with the gray of the water,
Spilling upward to the gray of the sky.

III

Therefore, my father, teach me your satisfaction and delight.
I have searched already through the leftovers in books,
      through the records of old friendships and new friendships,
      through receipts from the dynamo of the present—
I have examined the nicks and bangs on the painted stairs
      to my house,
The torn corner of my borrowed shirt,
The stains where the clumsy or misunderstood made their mark,
      smiling and desperate at a holiday bash,
I have examined the nicks, bangs, tears and stains
      on my own body,
Which remains even as it continues to occur.

I have been searching for the satisfaction of the swing,
      which also has no consequence,
      which moves without a journey,
      which from its mired posts dangles small creatures:
In them, origin and end and the dust of the stars.

PRESENTS

I always brought you irises, didn't you notice?
Cut to the quick, wilting even so

Cosmos, roses, whatever blooms in August
Nasturtiums in their season, herbs in theirs

Rosemary, fresh—once—dried, so many times
Bittersweet, its berries manic orange

Green-and-tarnish eucalyptus branches
Holly for cheer, pressed snowdrops following,

Perishing; I brought you irises and left
You nothing, really, not a sign of me.

QUAKING ASPEN

Populus tremuloides
Trembling Aspen
Golden Aspen
flyleaf
Are they not pure ecstasy, the Holy Ghosts of America?

I. A Reading from the Book of Old Shouters

Today I heard the testifiers, and knew them in their parts:
    flashing white and green, a sawtooth code of hands
    foolscap their skin, receptive to signs and letters
    rapid their sap to quicken, equally quick to die
All day preaching in explosions of minutes.

They publish God, these trees of North America.
They testify to a continent's soul:
    naturally prodigal, naturally radical,
    embracing terrain from chin to groin,
    dandled on the knees of Rocky Mountains,
    pioneering Saskatchewan,
    oblivious, precarious, exuberant,
    deciduous and therefore spiritual,
    settling quick as Yankees, displaced in turn by pine.
They publish and testify before the doubters, the frowners upon
    mobility.
They publish and testify before the evergreens denying
    the afterlife its winter of place.

O hearken to the aspen, you slow conifers, hesitating
    until the way is clear,

Hearken, dwellers in artificial tongues of light, idols
    gilding the midnight desktop,
Hearken, dwellers of Phoenix and Vegas
    where no trees prepare the way,
Hearken, dwellers in the green air of the conditional present
    when no sun, no moon inflames or punctuates,
They come before you with yellow alarm.
They publish and drop leaf.
They habilitate themselves.

II. THIRD SUNDAY IN ORDINARY TIME

These are directions for childhood in woodlands.
You'll need a hot iron, waxed paper, newspaper—
in Iowa, try *Des Moines Register* or similar.

Placing a leaf between sheets of waxed paper, and
placing waxed paper between sheets of the *Register*,
listen for rustles while reading the headlines:

"Klingensmith Triumphs in State Wrestling Tournament."
Iron at low heat until the wax incrassates,
sealing the leaf, and the crinkly noise stops.

You are compiling reliquiae: relics of
cottonwood, poplar, roundwood for decency,
oak, elm, box elder, black walnut, white birch,

catalpa for grace, silver maple for fortitude,
honey-haired locust, an almoner willow,
and aspen for last—the flyleaf, the homily.

Trim the excess. Look out at the darkening
branches of trees. Night overtakes dinnertime.
Soon snow will fall on the skeptical conifers.

Sliding it out from the warm newsprint pages—
fantastical teeth trapped between frosty papers—
remember the patter of planes caught in windsnap,

a visual music of alternate endings,
centrifugal impulses stemmed in your fingers,
heart shape that signals impossible creeds.

III. RESPONSORIAL PSALM

For it was written by the first Quaker, the itinerant Fox:

Be patterns (And verily thou art patterned of decoupage and
    pinking shears.)
Be examples in all your countries, places, islands, nations,
    wherever you come (And so to creekside, cranny and steep.)

That your carriage and life may preach among all sorts of people
    and to them. (How democratic thou art, widespreading
    and yellow with fervor.)

Then you will come to walk cheerfully over the world, answering
    that of God in every one (O pantheistic vibrato of leaf!
    Confetti in shudders!)
    Whereby in them ye may be a blessing and make the witness
    of God in them to bless you. (Shalom. Shantih. Amen.)

IV. CLOSING HYMN AND SPRINKLING OF ASHES

Do you hear, inconsolable one? You ask for exception,
    a singular message, one that will apply only to you.
I cannot give it; I have no particulars, no pamphlets that shake
    from the bones of aspen;
my catholic whispers do not satisfy.

22

It is always the putting forth, leaving, the coming after;
    displacement of originals;
always the dying who condole with us;
    always the dead who bring more life:

Here lie the native-born, restless and white-ribbed,
    who shiver, envision, die back in spasms,
and leave us, unsettled, surviving the winter.

VIENNA, I DON'T LOVE YOU

It's a dark hour when the glimmering hits.
Your jaggedy eyes shatter, the screech of glass

cascading to the sunk courtyard. Streetside
a happener-by hears, stiffens, proceeds.

She has come. Her body reeks damp sprigs.
Unsought she brought it, packed up in forgiving

moss. She sweeps your room; sprays iris wishfuls.
She trails rosemary strewn on the bed path.

You fold up after your retreating eyes.
It's too deep to gather her. You drop through

her creeping arms. *Please.* Too dark, say no—*please.*
Vienna, I don't love you any more.

You groan like crumpled foil. Folded, you fit
into the cupboard you cried in as a child.

ii

FEEDING FRENZY

From shore I see the splotch of turgid brown
on gray, above it the spray of commas: terns

who dart and drop wing, gravitating down
to bloody scraps they'll scavenge from the churn.

Bluefish in a frenzy feed with packed
malice, razor fins, devouring speed.

Schooled, doomed bait fish neatly turn and tack.
Their death throes are tiny. Invisibly they bleed

into that mass of bodies, loose-linked, floating
like a raft, except when breakers flash

a catch of scale, each longhand roll exploding
in war, a ravenous line, a scribbled blue thrash.

I root for mean fish, wheel to snatch the word
for hunger they disgorge from the chum-flecked surge.

104°

In the name of July the heat banks and turns like a lift of
    sparrows.
In the name of the lion-bearing month, it swaggers;
We can do no work in the face of it; we are overcome in its welter.
We the city-makers, the furnace-stokers, the curious,
    the experimenters;
We the utmost strainers, puncturing the planet's blue haze;
    relentless movers, persistent and wonderful;
We the scrawlers on rocks, clay, bark, parchment, canvas, paper,
    palimpsest, gold, markers on all things inkable and
    impressionable, are stopped.
We halt at this blister of heat.

The heat clasps us in its gloriole arms and leads us club-footed,
    our bones as telephone poles;
It drums out the buzzing, crackled insects (cheerless
    glockenspiels, clackers and cowbells,
        pried and shaken from the balding earth!)
In the name of July, the heat exacts live songs from skeletons;
    even the grasses must contribute their whir.
For July brings forth lions into August; even in heat is tribute
    required.

(But spare us, spare us! Our bellows are dry!
We cannot render unto thee, it is too hot.
See, a deathly cessation has come upon us like a winter.)

July sends mirages cascading; aurora borealis on the highway's
    yellow stripe.
They cascade in arcs, beaded and shirred;

They blind us, mirrors of our watery thoughts, our wavering
     clarity, the speechless sheen on unminted words;
They vanish even as we train our dazzled gaze upon them;
The black road shows through barren and soft.

July maddens us to stillness; we can give it nothing,
And even then it emanates in sea-fan waves.
The heat advances; it exhausts itself not.
In our drifting we feel its eternal compliance, gentle, horrible,
We know it will never cease waving; we know it is rooted and
     serene in the oceanic proportions of perpetual July.

Or does it not desire to be free? Or does it not seek, too, a death?
Does not this heat whelp gold husks like lions?

Then is this hot breath the giant exhale of a beast, a splintered
     century proceeding uncollected;
Then at its indraw does the lioness' belly tighten that, tapping,
     it may animate and percuss, bits jumping to its violence.
Then does it resemble hope, this breath, for it seeks
     improbable effect;
Then must we breathe in its hope, for we, too, are inspired;
Then must we crack our bellows, quicken stiff coals for their idle
     possibilities:
Quick, man the forge, fossils, and blow! Blow, before the last
     sparks die,
And the dragonflies, gold heralds of our oppression, go out.

SONNETS OVERHEARD IN SOHO

I. ALL I WANTED WAS A FIVE-CENT COPY

Denied a goddamn nickel's worth of service;
denied by jammed Manhattan, land of oh
sure, we can get it; Tuesday, business hours—
you tell me why the copy shop is closed.
I bump the door, blink at it, rattle the knob,
a sudden tourist of the afternoon.
Yet there are other copy shops, I think.
Bright yellow "5¢ Copy" signs festoon
my mind like phantom daffodils in fields
I know not where—illusions brightly wet
as taxis occupied by the wide-awake
on rainy days when you have overslept.

Ginkgoes lean, kicked by a wet-leaf breeze:
trenchcoats slapping thin commuter trees.

II. WHY CAN'T THEY LOOK IT UP? I ALWAYS DO

Forgive me and my kedged perpendicle,
I mumble at the cell phone bearer's approach.
I'm blocking traffic on this narrow walk.
Where's my knack of weave, duck, never touch?
My urban grace? Unglued, ungrafted, gone,
these fixtures, jimmied shelves on every square
inch of open wallspace—they've collapsed,
felling their houseplants, books and eveningwear

30

in massy chokes, exposing secret tunnels:
architecture built of disrepair.

So what if I look that strange man in the face
and lick his long brown dusty eyelids bare?
He looks but does not see me. Mercy, man,
your shortcut leads you past my full-blown plans.

III. EACH TIE COSTS $135

Stop! Consider! I'm standing at a church
where, once a year, the people bring their pets
before the brothers, shuffling up like me
to Houston Street, that Rover might be blessed.

Inside, sky blue snows down like ticker tape,
the blue of milk, of grace, pilaster blue
in code for old Italian parishes.
(The Irish never got it right, that hue.)

A souped-up Virgin Mary waves brightly
from her high niche. She says, "Enough, come clean."
Saint Anthony chimes in: "and bring your hamster!"

I start, but the door is locked, a policy
of crime prevention. Hey. It wasn't me.
The rats of SoHo, they go "see, see, see."

IV. NOT ONLY DID SHE LOSE HER JOB, BUT—

Who points that finger? Dismisses me? Demands?
It is my grandmother, with her metal laugh,
her luscious ferns, her stern piano, hands
that jerk like knitting needles, spirographs
even, her gestures, so elaborate—
like playing a harp.

31

At Grandpa's wake she led
the rosary. She knelt and laid her cheek
on his medicine chest. She patted down his dead
good suit. Her bitten unstrung rose beads clacked
staccato flight through damper-pedal talk
and complicated fingers. Rose beads clambered
to the corners of his black piano box.

Did I laugh when Grandma's rosary burst?
It is my grandmother, assuming the worst.

V. SERVICE SAVED MY LIFE

From Queens the city looks like a myth, but here,
an ocean when you're in it, there's no view.
Urbanity, it does not signify,
nor broken rosary, nor shade of blue.

I offer up new evidence: a rusting
lobster in his tank. The lily bloom
that worked its way up stem, claw by white-
knuckled claw. Things halted, past tense, hewn.
I'd rather be them than how the dancer feels,
the spiked notes shuddering her limber bone,
her tendons bowing under passages,
her feet bleeding, her muscles pulsed with tone
as she is moved. I'd rather quell to serve
earth's long, low, vexing, vast imperfect swerve.

CUTWORM

Wherefore the cutworm, that consumeth not what he destroys,
That sunders below the leaf, that razes at the spindle,
    that severs the stem's base, disdaining to carry off the fallen?
Wherefore the reaping, when he harvesteth not?

To what divinity is he homage? what New World, Hun,
    this slow marauder of earthen banks?
He cares nothing for trophies of conquest, he forsakes them
    freely,
The foliage and plume of felled peppers he disregards.
His triumph is not the slump of eggplants and broad spinach,
His glory is not the slack arms of sweet peas, whose fingers loosen
    on the soil where they dropped (they furl
    to the morning sun, shedding green,
    no more enraptured of fences.)
He is the Contradictor. He brings death to new life.
He introduces the Bitter One's point of view.
He is Excrement, the servant of leavings.

He ends the world in icy trumpets of wrath; his god is angry
    and unkind.
His god has sent a worm to diminish us.

Or he is wit, its purpose to observe, slicing what comes before it,
    that we may start and laugh at its clean divide.
Then is his plunder our plunder.
Then is his nature on our behalf, for at our pleasure he cleaves.

Then is he legendary: Paul Bunyan, delighting in the axe.
He lays the blade against the pale throats of the seedlings,

He worships their slight bodies, their top-heavy heads,
He sees they have not yet learned to stand straight, unquivering,
    he topples them at their very foot.

Let us praise and thank the cutworm, for he is joyous.
He has shown us the secret lure of the vandal.
Let us praise and thank him for epic excess.
Let us praise his wastefulness.

Without him, the endless wild grape would astonish us,
    its panic of length overgrowing sensible oak,
Without him, we would wonder too long at the also
    unfathomable path of swallows, their swift
    choices of flight, obliquities leaving us no trail,
    no wake.

ALMOST SUMMER HEAT

Maybe it's the smell of sweaty asphalt,
winded laughter bouncing off cement,
or night air spiked with hot spaghetti that leads
me where I can't quite place myself to go—

Oh, those young legs lording their bruises!
Oh, the grooved oak seats of barely June!
Big-paned rattles of sunshine, yellow-squared
distraction falling across exhausted school shoes!

My heart has stumbled sixty-seven times
on tangled old promises of summer grass,
even in spring, before I could have known
how long and dry another August stretched.

This year my heart skips, my feet break free
like heat of almost summer, praising, spare—

HATS OF BROOKLYN

I board the 44 Limited.
Roily with maps I board it,
Distracted, cowed, anxious I board it, a glare of rigor mortis
    among the black folks,
White as wax among the regulars I board it,
For I am late,
For I am lost.

I wedge in to the driver's amusement, my jabbering *now? now?*
    absorbed by his calm.
A front-row grandmother ducks with reflexive tact,
Her pink skull flashes caution—no staring—her hair an unraveled
    sweater *my* dead grandmother knitted once and bestowed.
    (I picked it apart rather than wear it.)

A smolder of muscle tone bumps me aside; compacted she
    displaces me.
Her boyfriend slouches seatward, all plaits and pleached arms
    You are not welcome, no, says his hair
    You are not welcome, no, say his arms
They speak to me, they tell me thus: I am the central event
    of this city bus.

(Do I believe hair braided days ago growls at last,
    its purpose fulfilled?
Do I believe arms cross at me, at me?
Then I am the coffin at a wake: I cannot blend in with the living,
    I will not blend in with the living.
O solipsism of the freshly dead!
No one can stop staring; finally I am—irresistible!)

I look back at the stares, and now I see:
The smoldering girl is late, too, and on her way
        to an unpleasant chore
The boyfriend, towed behind, coerced, nervous—or lost, ah!
I recognize my braided sweater, furious arms, impotence
        on a rock-hard love seat, hard as this city-bus seat,
In the cold parlor where I await my piano lesson.

Those were cold fingers, soon to poke the slick white keys
        (the black ones still unlearnt)
A cold metronome, an unyielding scale,
And judgment, my grandmother, the coldest.

This bus is warm with breath and bodies,
        my talent, secure,
My belief, revised to suit myself.

And out the window, men in hats, in extraordinary
        grizzly-bear hats, Hassidim, perhaps?
Long-coated, black-suited, black-shod, hairy men in hats!
White, white men in deep black hats!
In drifts they ponder down the sidewalks,
They stand in copses, in twos, threes, fives,
They hobnob with yarmulkes, tall, brimmed felt homburgs,
        they deign to the women's kerchiefs,
They blend in not at all, these fur capitals.

I try to name the hats; they defy me:
        their shape belonging to car-wash rollers
        their status conferred upon certain elderly males
        their occasion a Shabbat of unknown renown
        their quiddity the talismanic slap of braids—
I sit, I stare on the 44 Limited; I sit, revising myself.

This black world on a bus chartered through Brooklyn
        slides on by Williamsburg's hats
Intact like the Gowanus Canal, believing itself with me wrapped
        inside it,
And I am pearl-inciting sand, or a fingernail in need of paring,
Or the difference practice makes.

SIOUX GONE, NO ONE'S HOME

The prairie night is not like anywhere.
Never a house nearby. No sidewalks trimmed in

windows. No streetlamps spitting out light in brimming
circles for public use. No rapid flights of stairs.

The prairie trammels and stomps. It hunkers down,
mounching laps of grass, blown husks, what's left

of dry brown blood in dry Midwestern towns
where tough guys give and weak guys get.

Here or there the plain fumbles a building. House.
Pawn shop. Seed-corn dealership. No watchtower

to stave off coyotes lean for dogmeat snatched
from the sea of dry, dry grass that coughs like cows.

The bars fill weekly with hard-caked mud-hocked boots.
Through flat of night the decimated herd still moves.

ON AN ECCENTRIC LADY WHO TURNED HER APARTMENT INTO AN ARBORETUM

There's will at play, I'm certain, and desire;
a unified imagination speaks
of God knows what, or why, or even how
she got behind that wall of leaf and bole.

Like mixing peat with dirt to get the right
sub-tropical conditions into a pot,
she has concocted expertise of sorts:
life behind a wall of leaf and bole.

I spy a furtive bloom of cyclamen,
notorious fainter, sneaking off to die;
it's taken root there, in her tricky soil.
She got behind that wall of leaf and bole

and dug herself a nice, hospitable grave,
I think—though who's to say she hasn't found
the destiny we're all designed to have,
back there behind that wall of leaf and bole?

Our toes, so loose, so shy inside their socks,
may yearn for permanence and steady length.
There's vertigo: it recommends the earth,
our fortress earth, that ball of leaf and bole.

And how many dry nights have I waited
for replenishment, a long-haired offshoot

turning, turning toward your sometime light?
I might as well be made of leaf and bole.

I see her point, strange lady of the trees.
I find it hard to leave my living room
these days, what with the sidewalk bucked and gasping
"get thee behind a wall of leaf and bole!"

Yes, even fresh-poured concrete, the finest May
on record, streets cordoned off from cars
can crisp my narrow foot, my wilted sole.
I'll get behind a wall of leaf and bole.

THE BROOKLYN MUSEUM

The Museum's collection of decorative arts is considered one of the most important in the country. A pioneer in the installation of period rooms, the Museum now has 28 on exhibition, ranging from a 17th-century Brooklyn Dutch farmhouse to a 20th-century art deco library designed by Alavoine of Paris and New York.
from the Brooklyn Museum of Art's website

These are the homes, the homes of America,
    broken, rebuilt in the Brooklyn Museum.
I reach them upstairs, for they abide upon the fourth floor.
They assemble there, occupying it fully.

These are the homes of America; they speak in many voices:
Of upright Boston the townhouse;
The brownstoned mansion of a merchant's vain atrocity,
The eldest one rasps, a Dutch grange, low and cross-beamed,
They thunder or pipe the sprawl of our habitats, displantations
    cobbled on an improvised street.

I tour them alone, the homes of America.
My companion is missing, she is not here,
    nor did we arrange to meet in this place
But I, foster-child of myriad addresses, have wandered;
I of apartments grown too close or dear and therefore abandoned,
    of sublets in unsatisfying boroughs,
        of tossed garrets, left by looters in a disarray beyond
            indigence,
        of leases seized by implacable landlords and malicious
            landlords,

of abodes relinquished in collapses of the heart, hence of
        oscillating commitment and its attendant impermanence,
of quick judgment,
I of no fixity, headlong, squandering, modern,
I tour these exhibitions of constancy, that I might tremble
    at their thresholds.

> *Once real families lived in these rooms.*
> *They came to these chairs by night, by fire.*
> *A man sat reading from Bible or broadsheet*
> *aloud to the knitter's yarn-spitting metronome.*
> *Flames wrote large the shadow of granny's stooping*
> *and rocking; candles' sputtered light belied*
> *the soot above them, saying, not I, O Lord, not I.*

O evictions of former age!
O ousted ones, who once discharged your shelter unremarked,
How do you take it that I poke among you, squint into your
    wavering panes, duck under lintels?
How do you bear my glimpse around doorways?

I seek the peripheries of vanished lives, the living and dying
    in the houses.
I seek the last known address.

> *In his father's echo he lived concretely, one of the last.*
> *His buzzer'd steel door on N. Moore Street leads*
> *us to our own ideas of home: some glean*
> *dried flowers in their arrangements, some, the walls*
> *papered chintzy, some, spare terra cotta dotted with art objects*
> *or green casements unlocked in springtime,*
> *a bed throw carefully laid across a quilted spread—*
> *but never are there grannies in our dreams,*
> *or candles to throw rocking stooping shadows.*

These are the homes, the homes of America,
Their occupants dead who once poked at the threshold
    or passed it quickly or stumbled across it backward, crying
    no, wait—

Their neighbors, daughters, sons gathered afterward.
Their people marked death's passage with stones and crosses
And chose for the bones some obvious resting place,
    a farm or churchyard leaching nutrients,
For each had his sod then, his parcel and people; even in death
his foundation was known.

I think on a young man, the son of a president,
prominent of family—surely he is known,
yet his death poses uncertainties, of how
to mark it, and where. For there is Hyannisport
less loved, and Arlington most martial and unfit,
High Mass at St. Ignatius (too far uptown,
besides, he never went to church) struck from the list.
Thus it is sidewalk we have chintzed and dotted
with objects; thus are his ashes at sea.

Where are the graves, the graves of our America?
They are not installed here, ready to be toured.
Where is our threshold, for our permanent crossings, and how—
    must we tiptoe or seep into the netherworld?
    must we be sucked through tubes by a machine?
    must we lift up, an abstraction like this age, migratory
        and primitive?

Here, in a hallway, I witness these homes.
They huddle over their old uses, yet insisting
    on blackened timbers and brick.
They enclose and display their atavistic hearths.
For the dead of past centuries are roped off here,
    and their knowledge, with them.
They cannot cluster in the whitewashed halls like ordinary
    townsmen in crisis;
They cannot congregate on a sidewalk, bringing with them
    spontaneous shrines.
Who calls upon them now to make quick decisions, unrehearsed?
Who dislodges them, and sends them back again?
O homes, dead homes of America, we come
    ourselves displaced to tour thy gallant hollows.

ASSASSINS IN LOVE

Gleam of night, Contrarian City! Prowler,
Hulked One, Switchblade piercing the Hudson current!
Sweep your back-street promises to an ingrate,
Me in my small sleep:

Give me dreams, I'll wake them before they dry off
Give me filthy lucre, I'll squeeze it, sweetness
Give me kind intent as you find it hiding—
Gifts of the hit man.

All the night long, Cherokee Jeep alarms wail.
Limos double-park where the sleekly coiffed drink
Safely, knowing gizmos and drivers guard them.
Affluence bars them.

I will wake to terrible light, the litter,
Freaks adrift from yesterday's bacchanalia.
I can ask no more of this crime in progress:
Gotham, my chosen.

iii

THAW

I have planted too early, all my seedlings have drowned—
    they couldn't stand the rain's enthusiasm
And I, I couldn't bear to wait for spring to dry.
It does, I know, I wasn't lied to, but oh, I was intoxicated.

Blame the undeniable white of dogwood,
    blasting like an act of God onto the fallow lawns,
Blame forsythia wands for pointing their yellow, they direct me,
Blame how flagstones clean themselves of travel,
    they are so prepared and wise to eternal movement,
For the Judas tree clenches its fistfuls of pink snow,
For the tulip tree stretches its pale palms in supplication,
For crab apple and cherry bedeck their gnarled arms
    (they are not too old to give pleasure or receive pleasure,
    nor are they too callused to forget).

The seeds within me fluttered like eyelids, and spun and whirled,
    invisible as spores, important as spores,
And I could not wait to be invited, but sank my fingers forward
    into the sleeping clay.

ASH GROVE OF ASH

Shriver and shadow, my shade for good and ill,
you bend divulging branches. You stand clear
with narrow waist, clean-shirted. You nod, hearing.
You shelter me, too. You gather crossed blond quills

of saplings into fists, binding their violent
crouch and spring. You bathe taut knots, embalmer.
Now cool prevails on your pale green leaves, and calm
steeps your roots, quenching their crooked silence.

I see you are not mine, but reservoir
beneath the grove, distiller of rot, bog, bracken,
broken trees, the clear-cut past, its dying

brush that scudded like cut hair at your drying
channels, your wandering arms—*come back, come back,*
my root voice creaks of thirst, like a long shut door.

CAST STONES

And there is weeping and scratching of the face,
And there are the hoarse cries of the accused,
And her hair is wet, slapped across her cheek like kelp,
And there is the babble of curiosity, for life in the village
    is not without incident after all,
And here are the seven brothers, unmoved, with concrete chests
    like hulls filled with ballast;
They make no sound, neither cries nor whispers, but surround
    her with the confounding silence of inevitability.
And here is her father, eyes scanted.
For days he has seen only rocks and feet.
For days his ears have burned with rumors, rustles, murmurous
    lies, shameful imaginings in his forehead, burrowing.

And where is her mother? Where sisters?
Here is only torment, twisted like cloth, the loose corner of it
    a tent fly clapping.

It is too late for the crowd of watchers, they have undressed her
    already.
At the first news, they unwind her wrap, her veil,
At night they dream of her handled thigh, touching
    where they suppose other men touched,
At night they awaken at a puff of air: *is it you slipping into*
    my tent, barefoot and scented like a Roman?
Is it I whom you seek? Is it I, ardent ghost? Is it I,
Breath of my unchaste desire?
It is too late for these men, who have already possessed her
    and been possessed.

49

(But she has not been possessed, not daring.
She faltered in love with the curly-haired one, she twisted free
    of his warm skin, his salt and rough hands,
Fear dried her and made her run.)

Fear dries her still, turning her screams to a rattle in the throat.
She knows it does not matter what she dared or did not dare.
It does not matter now, accursed, to the myth-making village.

Here are the seven brothers and the father, moving like a galley
    up the hill.
Like galley men they flank her.
Like a wake the flange of watchers follow, tramping to view her,
    leaving the sand stamped with confusion.
They push uphill toward one who squats, waiting, also
    surrounded.
He writes with his finger in the warm sand;
He obliterates what he marks, then writes again;
He considers the scribes and the laws of the Hebrews;
    he fingers a commandment in the grasp of its exception.

LILIES OF GETHSEMANE

O lily, blood lily, don't shake your locks at me.
I have not faltered, nor have I complained,
and when I wept I did it in the grove
where no one else could see.

O lily, bent lily, why have you not revived?
There's water all around the flaming woods
where cardinals, catbirds, finches, even jays
collaborate with light.

O lily, dead lily, shake off your lethargy.
Not for you, the pride of parables
knowing tomorrow whose bloody locks will shake
and stud Gethsemane.

UNDER STARS

And I am flung apart, like carnival lights, like dice,
splayed so wide my arms embrace the lit-up sky,
its stars like nails—a first-time lover, not embracing.

Kissing my spine, my elbows, calves and shoulder blades,
the clumsy elder wood resolves itself beneath me.
It uplifts me. It gathers now, secure as dread.

My hands hold round red tokens. My feet are also red.
If played, my ribs would surely snap like rigged air guns.
Ratcheting up I ride, racked slow as a Ferris wheel,

clicking along to hit my pose: the famous dangle
over the dusty hill. The desultory crowd
below looks up at me, glittering, hoisted, most high.

I catch the sky tilting, disaster, splattering light,
the roll of celestial dice. Oh, how those crazy stars
I loved to kiss vault over my shocking bare crown.

SUMMER CHAPELS

Behold the summer chapels, the beach-side steeples, the prayer
    shacks,
Behold the houses of salt-air Sundays,
Behold makeshift religion, and praise it.

Never was marble here, or gilded apse, but behold the rafters
    that shoulder the nave,
Praise the clapboard, the plain wood floors,
Praise all forms low-key and makeshift.

Praise all parishioners, for they, too, are low-key and makeshift:
    the unpracticed choir, singing in hesitant accord,
    the cumbersome entrances, none to his usual pew,
    the peering halts of the late-to-Mass,
    the prayerful mumbles, catholic, from city to city
        universally paced—
    though they walk to the altar out of step, yet
        do they recite in unison, these strange mouths
        eased into familiar rhythms—
O praise them all, the strange and the familiar!

Praise bikini straps showing through creased blouses,
Praise those who forgot to pack dress shirts; they lower their
    heads to bright tees,
Praise bright tees, that exalt volleyball gear and accounting firms
    and juice,
Praise shoes and sandals of every ilk,
Praise the motley, side by side with the made-up,
    the sure-voiced with the bewildered
    the ramshackle with the sleek
    and the regular with the new, all praise.

There are no more sea captains here, alleluia.
The whalers and shrimpers are become card-shop owners,
      alleluia.
Old superstitions are dry-docked now, alleluia, and forgotten.
Gone are the prayers of fair weather, bountiful catches, safety,
Gone are the widows who chant in the front pews, their jaws
      like pumps (how long they pumped the air
      whose prayers had been washed up bloated,
      or swept overside, or drowned, unanswered!)
Gone the string of wrung-out old men who doze in back,
      mouths almost open,
Gone the great middle of baitfish, the boys and girls as old
      as they are young,
Gone the town drunk, and the town slut, alleluia,
All hail the summer worshippers, the mosaic of worshippers,
      stained and dappled are they, and tolled.

HIS ARID WAYS

Dandelion-style my tough heart grows
gladly in the worst of places, succumbing
to every passing mower as he mows.
I ride his blade's quick mercy. At its hum

my cut stalk bleeds an anesthetic milk. In
hours I'm cured. By week's end, white hair drifting,
I sow other hearts to graft their silken
roots on gravel, shooting their stems, uplifting

their rabid suns. Let us all re-enact
the indestructibility of weeds
who sprout in concrete, faces gone to seed,

no longer beautiful: no young man's slackened
ardor can blunt our optimistic blades,
for we have means to plumb his arid ways.

SMALE BYRDYS Y-STWDE

from a fifteenth-century cookery book

Most solemn and particular are the rites that render the stew,
And as the recipe begins in baptism, so doth the man.

I

*Take smale byrdys, an pulle hem an drawe hem clene, an washe
hem fayre*

And my brother took vows most solemn and particular,
    at birth unwitting, and again at twenty-five,
At twenty-five years he took his secular life, he found himself
    ordained.
Then most holy and unusual hath he become,
Then most transformed.

For he is deft in the ways of the Mass,
    his dazed hands clarify at its proceeding,
The baptized and confirmed leave him sure of their blessedness.
Therefore he weareth his collar at all times, even unto sleep,
And he crosseth not the street against the light,
    but ever follows its commands to walk
    and not to walk,

And his collar holds him from the throngs, and from me:
    for he offers to me a handshake in greeting
    he sees me, yet he sees not me;
    he offers extremities, as unto a stranger,
    for I am a stranger to him, or unclean.

(I cannot abide this dress and formal stare. I insist on our relation:
I bypass his token arm, I clasp him full to my body,
     I graze his shirking cheek with my bare one
And he receives my commination woodenly, swallowing it
     unremarked.)

I consider the multitudes within one saporous drop of stew:
The bonds of sweet and salt, the commingling of herbs
     with meat,
The intricate sequence of chemistries, each occurring
     in its particulars of heat, tempo and proximity,
And I consider how accidental are the origins of stew,
Yet how fixed becomes its legend.
I consider my brother, original, composed, and the birds therein,
     which are small.

II

*An schoppe of the leggys and frye hem in a panne of freysshe grece
ryght wyl*

The cathedral swells; it undulates with the robes of many birds:
     the cardinal cocking his mace,
     the smooth-skulled monsignors,
     the brown partridges of Saint Francis swaying
          in their rope belts,
     the common black grackle and redwing and crow of diligent
          pastors (they flock even as they tend),
     the flash of purple finch, gleaned from obscure and
          dwindling orders,
These pour and congregate on the limestone expanse
     for the ordination is at hand.

And the cathedral swells with music, also, and undulating chants
     and incense.
The seven novitiates (so many eyes on so few!) fall on their faces;
They rise and kneel, obedient to the legend;
They promise.

57

They accept finally the blessings of the initiated, the stew
    of robes:
From each robe a pair of hands is laid on each of the seven sworn,
And I am become wooden in the smoke and swirling noise,
    the unbearable procession of blessings,
For the cathedral is full of priests, and the hands go on forever.

Now a robin perches upon my deck, and stares,
And I see that it is fattened, and hath partaken of many stews
But it suspects no Other, hiding behind her screen door, thinking
    thus of stews
For a robin knows nothing of idle watching or speculation,
It steeps not in the mulled juice of legend,
Dreams not of ancestors, nor of their chopped legs, nor of its own
    chopped legs,
Considers not the origins of recipes.

III

Than lay hem on a fayre lynen clothe, an lette the grece renne owt

Here in the year of our Lord 1972 is a boy of ten,
Here is a baby sitter stirring at the stove,
Here will be a dinner set upon the table.
See the food of 1972 hath spilled its trinkets from boxes
    onto the stove,
And it is as unto an airplane model kit, and the cooking thereof
    is unto assembly.
And the sitter seeketh the envelope among pasta Legos
    or spaghetti Lincoln Logs:
The pouch of the powder magical she seeks, neon extract
    of a Fisher Price apothecary.
It will spring into sauce at the enchantment of water,
It will bind the dish and make tumid its shape,
It will render edible the unlikely.

The boy and his sister eat from paper plates;
There is no fair linen cloth.

For the America of 1972 eats from polymers and polyethylenes
    and the grease is not fresh as in the recipe
    and the decade is tumid with dogma and stale dreams
    its excess potential will not drain; uncalled-for hopes sit
    claggy and the sluggish juices will not run out.

The boy sees this and shakes.
At ten, the boy sees that there is no brilliance
    in the orange kit-food.
At ten, he dreams of finest fair linen.
At ten, he vows disobedience to what is,
    invisibly stocking what he will have be.

IV

Than take oynonys, an mynce hem smale, an frye hem on fayre frysshe
grece, an caste hem on an erthen potte

O riskers! Evolvers! O fugitives from caution!
O wonder of originality, its departures swift, its arrivals in new
                                             clothes:
    the Bard embarking from little Latin and less Greek
    the trembling finger trapped in the hulking unchiselled
        Michelangelo
    the scarecrow president poking out of his Illinois suit.

I look out upon my deck and consider the earthen pot, our planet,
And the large birds that have taken their historic arcs
And the small birds that have brought their small contributions,
    for who divined the pomegranate, how its tunnels of seed
        are good and nourishing?
    who dried, ground and watered to make dough of wheat?
    who appraised the yeast, so reluctant to explain itself?
    who delved into the spiny artichoke?
I consider these brave advancers, who saw bread in a flake of dust.

And my brother I consider at eleven, twelve, thirteen,
The years stretching long as shadow at day's death,
The hardening taste at the pit of his imagination.

V

than take a gode porcyon of canel, an wyne, and draw thorw a
straynoure, an caste in-to the potte with the oynonys;

And the boy sits in the playground reading.
In the shadow of the old brick schoolhouse he sits,
Studies the pages amid the din of four-square,
Looks not up at the see-saw of public opinion.

The boy sits reading, a cast on his leg, for it is broken:
    the playground hath broken his leg; yea, verily,
    the merry-go-round, pinwheeled and exuberant,
    hath snapped it for pure joy.
He sits in the recesses.
He hath retreated to the shadows of books;
    no troops follow him there.
The boy sits reading in the shadows, the cast on his leg gleaming,
    bereft of signatures.

VI

than caste the byrdys ther-to, an clowys, an maces, an a lytil quantyte
of powder pepir ther-to, an lete hem boyle to-gederys y-now;

O stew, thou art spiced darkly with politics, public school, class
    and geography.
Thou art flavored with small-town burghers; the farms
    surround you
(Yet he denies the earthen unguent of canel and wine)
O stew, thou art built of experience, games, propitiatory acts,
    but art contained always in our pot of ground.

        Come, little birds—but little more than bones,
        Thou legless, pale, skin-stippled specimens
        Of grief, forgotten not, but set aside—
        Come closer now. Come melt thy scanty meat.

Thou drawest fire; I absorb thy broth.
Tender up thy thyme, exhale thy graceful rue.

I consider how long the small birds have boiled together in the
    growing boy;
I judge it enough.

For it is 1985, and the boy is at the end of his college years
And he grows no more and is a boy no longer
And he faces the shadows, the reeling tilt of future dips and
    pivots,
And time, a white cast unwritten upon.

And I consider the graduate in his black robe, wooden,
    undistinguished among the many black robes.
His hands hide in the black folds; they have found a nest.
They appear only at the utmost greeting, to shake in the glare.
And the rites of the college are most solemn and particular
And the pinwheeling robes are soon manifesting their joy
And the merriment is as unto a playground
But my brother has found the shadows even here,
    and retreateth unto them,
And no fondness or friends pursue him; no memories come.

VII

*. . . than caste ther-to whyte sugre, an powder gyngere, salt, safron,
an serue it forth.*

And even as their thin bones settle to the bottom, the birds
    have long been eaten;
They are consumed in the making.
Before its origin the stew has been served forth.
In its recipe lies the taste of its absorption.

For at the center of the pot was grief—iron birth and death,
    our common disease—

61

At the center always was this sorrow.
No herb can disguise it; no powder dissolve.

For now have all foods been discovered and conjoined,
        the pomegranate and the artichoke, alas!
        the orange kit of pasta,
For now is left us only to simmer thereof in earthen pots
        familiar ingredients (cruel canel, or wine),
For the smallest birds stew in the fierce, deep juice,
Smallest ones, and freshest from the heartland.

VALLEY FORGE

September hints how frost will flank the air.
Breath no longer slinks away but turns
    and shows itself a ghost.
"Look there," a soldier says. It takes a beat
to see them buried, almost, in the mast:

crocuses push aside the rusting moss
and nettles with their pink-bullet blooms.
    "Deserters." They dodged the spring,
yet live by countermand: the order lodged
inside their bulbs, a cold, cold clemency.

"A foolish time they picked to hazard forth,"
he thinks, marching off to Valley Forge,
    just another campsite.
His upturned bayonet spears maple leaves
dropping, slain, their papery edges ripped.

Did they obey or choose today to die?
The high blue sky above them, coldly vital,
    will fail to depths of purple
as fighting gold and red (taxation! blood!)
prolific leaves fall uniformly dead.

Not much withstands an adulated slaughter
each year of blue, gold, red, except perhaps
    a band of crocuses
under the mulch, the marching feet, their bloom
the scar of winter's white-breath'd edge.

PATRIOTS OF AMERICA

Sodful, crew-cut, strict, victorious, edged,
the lawn unfolding obvious dots (impatiens,
geranium, zinnia, Sir!) is proud, is Right:
a much-too-perfect flag of red and white.

The bluesman plays a long and tattered stripe.
He may be loaded, but damn, his fingers go
free and high, all the way up river.
The ones who hear it know it with a shiver.

Summer muscles out another furl
of unpredictable straight lines and yells
like a visionary, curling and strong,
when Billie Jean beats Yvonne Goolagong.

A red fox digs a hole in the perfect lawn
chasing a pulse, and there's America:
spangled above, below, dark catacombs,
persistent voles and unsuspecting worms.

ANNE BRADSTREET'S FIRE

*Here Follows Some Verses upon the Burning of Our House
July 10th, 1666, Copied Out of a Loose Paper*

How American—
not fire burning down a house, but a poem
about fire burning down a house
(and not symbolically, either).

There's even rubbish in the poem, what's left
        after devastation
(good there's something after devastation).
Anne Bradstreet *by the ruins oft* did walk.

The whole town by the ruins oft did walk;
no better place for ash than where it burnt.
        The town walks by,
but only Mrs. Bradstreet writes the poem.

And, yes, she draws a moral from the flame.
She pulls it out, a pen, Excalibur—
        Or is it a shield?
Or palm tack like the saints used to impress

themselves that flesh is flesh, is only flesh,
        fire divine,
and folly all things tangible—remember,
Anne? *My pleasant things in ashes lie.*

Her places, too, have been consumed, the air
composed of where she always slept is there,
        but not there;
the burning roof has suctioned out whole rooms.

And when she greets her Father's house
although *with glory richly furnished*
    it seems bare,
as if it had been flattened, air let out,

as if the guests had left their bones behind,
had lost their pretext, their material,
    America.